Journey With
The Wagon Master

Joseph Newton Borroughs
1840-1919

First Printing
April 1998
© Earthen Vessel Productions

Text © 1997 Loretta Burriss Ussery
Originally written by
Joseph Newton Borroughs in 1911

Photos & Documents courtesy of
Loretta Burriss Ussery
and Joseph Newton Borroughs III

Editor: Carolyn Wing Greenlee
Layout & Design: Stephanie C. Del Bosco
Cover Layout & Design: Stephanie C. Del Bosco
Final: Daniel Worley

Cover Photo: *Wagon Train for Wildcats* (bluffs near Fort Bertold crossing the plains to Montana, Stereograph, 1866)
© Collection of The New-York Historical Society #67962
Used by permission

Library of Congress Cataloging–in–Publication Data
Borroughs, Joseph Newton, 1840–1919.
   Journey with the wagon master / Joseph Newton Borroughs.
      p.   cm.
   ISBN 1-887400-16-8 (pbk.)
   "Originally written by Joseph Newton Borroughs in 1911"—T.p.
verso.
      1. Overland journeys to the Pacific. 2. Borroughs, Joseph Newton,
1840–1919—Journeys—West (U.S.) 3. West (U.S.)—Description and
travel. 4. West (U.S.)—Biography. 5. Coaching—West (U.S.)—
History—19th Century. 6. Frontier and pioneer life—West (U.S.)
I. Title.
F593.B73   1998
917.804'33—dc21   98-24324

Earthen Vessel Productions, Inc., Kelseyville, California, USA

Journey With The Wagon Master

Joseph Newton Borroughs

Earthen Vessel Productions

Table of Contents

Introduction

This is the story of fourteen year old Joseph Newton Borroughs and his older brother, the Wagon Master Lewis Chamblee Borroughs and their wagon train journey across the continent.

For Lewis, this was his fourth trip as a Wagon Master on treks west leading covered wagon trains. For Joe, it was his first. He was to spend his fifteenth and sixteenth birthdays on the trail driving a wagon, observing and storing up memories, for years later, he was to write the story of this trip.

It was a slow journey of two years, as they spent two winters at different locations on the trail amassing a herd of cattle to drive west and to have new wagons made for the emigrants joining the train for California.

This journal was nearly lost to our family. My Aunt was a court stenographer and had borrowed it to have copies made. Somehow she forgot about it and, years later when I asked about it, she didn't know where it was. Several months later, after much searching, she found it lying on a shelf in the judge's chambers.

This story is important. It is part of history for all of us and the story of two brothers who, in different ways, shared a journey of emigrating people coming to California, people who would be seeing the Pacific Ocean for the first time.

~Loretta Burriss Ussery

Editor's Notes

Joseph Newton Borroughs wrote this account fifty years after his westward journey. We were so entertained and impressed by his storytelling skills that we decided to present his account as an unedited primary document with its charming humor and the spelling and punctuation of the day, though there were some obvious typographical errors which we did not feel we needed to preserve.

Of the thousands of people heading West, some never made it. Some limped their way there and grieved their losses all their lives. Some embraced the challenge and reveled in the new land. Pioneer diaries, letters and journals reveal a mosaic of personalities in a vast variety of circumstances, opportunities, and adversities. It has always interested me to see what they did to meet them. What kinds of personalities did they have? What attitudes? What fortitudes? What principles? What character was built? What beliefs and philosophies held them steady? What motivations failed? Joseph Newton Borroughs made it with style, and lived accordingly the rest of his long and productive life. Within his lavish supply of words, perhaps you may discern your own understanding of the source of his strength and delight.

~ Carolyn Wing Greenlee
Editor

Dedicated to my grandfather,
Joseph Newton Borroughs.

~ Joseph Newton Borroughs III

Legend

✗ Start of Journey, September 7, 1854 in South Carolina, most likely Anderson County

♦ Visit with brother George in Georgia, most likely Chamblee Georgia, town named after family

✳ Winter quarters 1854 on the Little Black River on the border of Arkansas and Missouri

✚ Winter quarters 1855 in Lafeyette County, Missouri, main leg of journey started here May 7, 1856

■ Old Fort Kearney

★ Location of cattle rustlers trial & execution

▲ Carson Canyon and Sierra Nevada crossing

● End of journey September 13, 1856, in Sacramento California

Approximate Route
Lewis Chamblee Borroughs' Wagon Train
(1854 –1856)

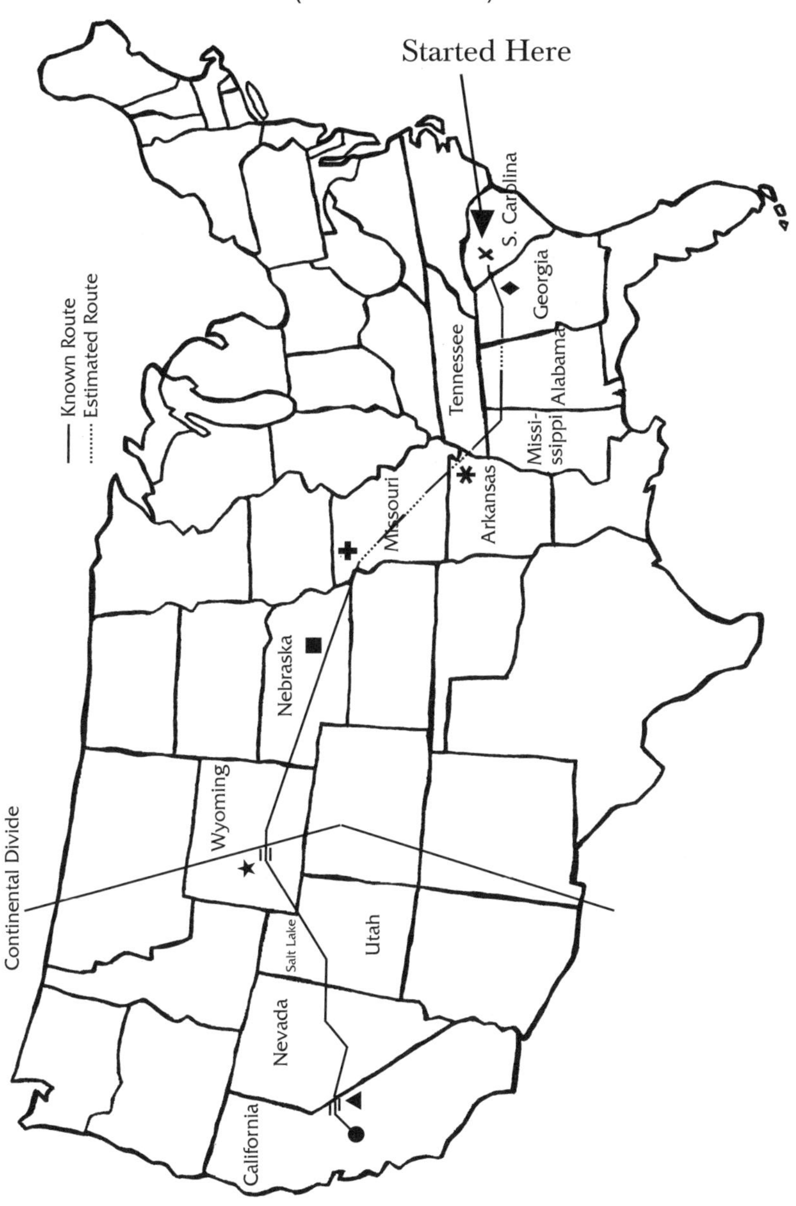

Journey With The Wagon Master

Chapter I

"How would you like to go to California with Lewis?"

These were the words addressed to me, by an older, motherly sister one morning as I sat by the fireside in my father's home.

I was then a boy in my fourteenth year. Lewis was an older brother, a man doing for himself before the days of my first recollection.

This, however, is not to be a family history; but a reminiscent account of my trip to California. The remark of my sister was the first intimation I had that any one but myself ever thought of such a thing as my going to California. Brother Lewis had already made three trips across the "Great American Desert", as it was then called; the first one being in 1849. I also had another brother, James, far west, California, by water, but who died of cholera almost upon his arrival. But ever after I had an unceasing desire, and fully intended at some future time to see the Golden State, though had never mentioned it to my most intimate friends.

But when sister Eliza put the question above to me, a suspicion arose in my mind that, somehow, the question of my going with Lewis was being discussed in the family, and my reply was:

"O I wish I could!"

Then began the most earnest persuasion of her mind and heart against my thinking even of such a thing. All the difficulties, dangers, trials and possible sufferings of the journey, together with what then seemed an almost endless distance, by which I would be separated from all the other members of the family; also the almost certain and near-heartbreaking homesickness with which I would be attacked; together with every other argument she could think of, was brought to bear upon me. However, the old saying of "water on a duck's back" would have been very applicable, so far as the effect in restraining my desire to undertake the journey went. Indeed, to use another of like classical character, it "added fuel to the fire."

I found out, though, from her, that the subject of my going was under consideration by my Father and brother. This, of course, doubled, if possible, my boyish desire to cross the plains, see the sights on the way and on the west coast of our great country. The pleadings of my sisters were continued from time to time, even up to the morning of our departure, which was the 7th of September, 1854.

I wish here to serve timely notice that my leaving my home was in no sense because it was not a good home. As I sit today writing, and think, as I have doubtless a thousand times before, I cannot recall a single element that was wanting to make mine a perfectly pleasant, and desirable home in every particular. I do most certainly think no boy ever entertained more profound respect and love for his father than I did for mine, poorly as I may have shown it, and as much as I may now regret my failure to have done so.

No, it was just my boyish, and in some respects thoughtless desires to ramble and satisfy my curiosity to see and know what was beyond the bounds of my home life. And this, as with all other boys in those days and that country, was quite limited.

The Home Leaving

That seventh of September morning will, I think, be among the last things fading from my memory. I had seen my beloved Father stand beside the death bed of a dear sister of mine, and never a tear dimmed his eyes, and I wondered with great childish wonder why, when everybody else was weeping bitterly. I learned later why, by hearing him say to some friends, that the great sorrow of his life was that he could not find relief for an over burdened heart in tears, like other people.

But on that September morn, when he came to take the parting hand with his baby boy, there were tears in his eyes and upon his cheeks; and it required all my boyish desires for travel and sight seeing in strong exercise, to prevent my getting off my horse and refusing to go. I had somehow managed to say good-bye to the other members of the family, my stepmother and sisters, each of whom I loved with all my boyish affection, with a fair degree of courage, but this was my Waterloo. I could hide my tears no longer, and wept freely, somewhat, at least, to the relief of a burdened heart.

But we were off, and soon, with new sights, and a boy's native talent for throwing off trouble, my sorrow soon passed away. For was I not really on the road to California, and were there not before me the great plains and mountains and Indians and what not to be seen and known? Surely mine were great opportunities.

So in the space of about twelve miles, we crossed the river, at that point the dividing line between my native state of South Carolina, and Georgia; and I was on entirely new territory. And already I began to feel quite the traveler for one of my age, which wanted from that time to the twenty-fifth of December to carry me to my fifteenth year.

Georgia Events

Quite a number of trivial, though to us interesting things took place on our way through this state.

I forgot to mention that Mr. J. M. Stevenson, the son of a neighbor of my Father's, was going with my brother to California, also, an almost unpardonable oversight this on my part, for he was an excellent man and was my brother's partner in buying stock to drive across the plains.

There was at that time a brother of mine, older than Lewis, brother George, who was living in Georgia. Our first point was to make him a short visit for a few days on our way. We reached his home, as I now remember, on the third day. A discovery I soon made was, that chestnuts which were now rapidly ripening, were quite abundant on his farm. I managed to collect quite a lot for munching on the road, as we did not stop for lunch at noon time; and that was quite a new and undesirable experience for one who, as I did, always managed to have with him a good sized appetite, which generally began to make its wants known about 11 o'clock in the forenoon.

Lewis left Brother George's the day before Mat. (Mr. Stevenson) and I did, to attend to some business off our line of travel. When Mat. and I started the next day, somewhat earlier than usual, this appetite of mine began putting in its claims, and I undertook the contract of meeting said claims with chestnuts. And although warned by my companion that my frequent draughts might not only cause the return of unpaid future checks, but also prove disturbing to the business of the new place of deposit, I continued to make quiet and sly calls for further amounts until all claims were satisfied.

Sure enough about 3 P.M. the new bank of deposit began entertaining protests. And these were to the effect that the natural course of business was becoming badly cramped, and that, as a result, the depositor would have to stand the damages. And I found that, under the law governing in the case, the protestant could make good his claim. The verdict rendered was: "Chestnuts in abundance in this case was chestnuts too abundant." And as penalty I was held in *durance vile* for the sum of four hours; or from 2 P.M. 'til 6 P.M., when I was released under promise of future good behavior.

Anyhow my appetite failed to put claims for further supplies for several hours subsequently.

It was after a long day's ride, the next day, with but little breakfast and no dinner, with refusal of entertainment for the night at a number of farm houses, we finally arrived some time after dark at one Mr. Buffington's, who kindly took us in.

The family having had supper, of course, we took our meal with none of them present. It was a good meal, too, with but one objection to be found. Of course, we were all quite hungry and I felt as if on the near edge of starvation, as I had been the better part of two days without anything that "stayed my stomach" the right way.

Now, the objection mentioned was to the biscuits. Not that they were not good, for they were. They were altogether too good for their size. While there was not complaint from them, there was considerable hard feeling for them, when the negro girl who was waiting on the table knocked over the candle (coal oil lamps were yet unbegotten) and put it out; and while gone to light it, I at one end of the long supper table, asked Lewis to pass the biscuits, of which the girl had just placed on the table a bountiful supply. When the plate reached me, I appropriated all that one hand could hold, and might have used the other, but Lewis had withdrawn the plate on call from Mat. at the other end of the table, who adopted the policy I had introduced, to prevent the frequent calls on Lewis to "Please pass the biscuits."

Perhaps the most important occurrence in this state was the purchase of a small lot of cattle, some twelve or fifteen head, as I remember, to drive more than three thousand miles to California, a feat performed, perhaps, by no other bunch of cattle in the United States; and every one of them made the entire trip!

But this has already grown beyond due proportions, and so I close to tell the story further in the next.

Chapter II

Crossing the line into Alabama, we arrived at the home of our uncle by marriage, and Hall by name, where we spent three or four days, putting the cattle in pasture.

Being of an inquisitive nature, I soon discovered what, to me, was a curiosity. Pouring out of the end of a hollow log some six inches in diameter, was a stream of beautiful, clear, cold water. As I looked along its length, I saw the end of that log was stuck into the end of another, and that into another, until I lost sight of them in the brush up the side of the mountain, at the foot of which my uncle lived.

Two things puzzled my inquiring mind, one of which at least I thought I could solve, and that was where that water came from. So I followed the line of logs up the mountain a quarter of a mile perhaps, and found the end of the last log in a fine large spring. And this solved mystery number one, namely, how a spring hundreds of yards up a mountain side could be down at the house. But this did not touch the solution of the next and greater one; how so many fine poles or logs of the same size could be found with the hearts rotted out, for that was all the way I could see the matter. But the answer to my question as to how it was left me in the same condition as was the lady who asked a man minus a leg how he was so unfortunate as to lose it. The gentleman, tired perhaps of answering that question so many times, replied: "Well, Madam, I will tell you if you promise me to ask no further question about it."

The lady, of course, promised she would not.

Said he, "It was bitten off."

After thinking a while, she said: "Well, I promised I would ask no further questions and I won't, but I declare I would like to know what bit it off."

They told me the holes were bored. I had not promised to ask no more questions, but having been laughed at for supposing the heart had rotten out, I thought silence the better part of wisdom in the case, so I said no more.

I learned the second evening that we were to have a fine treat next day. About two miles south from Uncle's home was a large cave in the mountain, and we were to visit it. So about ten o'clock the next morning, with candles, matches, lunch and a drinking cup, we went to the cave's mouth.

As memory now serves me, this opening was ten or twelve feet high and almost as wide.

After entering a few rods, the light from the opening growing dim, we lighted a candle. Soon we could see on the side of the cave, which widened at places to a hundred feet or more, other openings, which, on examination, proved entrances to rooms, some larger and some smaller; some with walls smooth and perpendicular, others rough and slanting. Some of these openings were large enough to allow one to crawl through them, and others were quite small. About a fourth of a mile farther we came to the first stalagmites and stalactites. Some of these were clear as crystal, while others were colored by the soil carried in the drippings forming them. In one place they had met and joined together, forming a pillar from floor to ceiling. The cave made quite short turns at a place or two and there we left burning candles, lest on our return we should take some of the openings leading away from the main cave and thus get lost.

We finally came to where the cave seemed to end; but on looking we found an oak pole some twenty feet long leaning against the wall. This had evidently been used as a kind of stairway minus the steps, as it was worn quite smooth from use. This we climbed and found the cave larger than on the lower floor. There were not so many side rooms, nor any stalagmites nor stalactites on this floor. In all we must have gone a good half mile from the entrance. On looking up at this point, one could see a faint streak of light from above, but there was no way of reaching this ceiling, as it was a hundred feet or more from the floor. We then returned to the lower floor, and to a large spring or pool, which, on testing, we found was fine drinking water, and ate our lunch, as it was about one o'clock. After resting we examined a number of the rooms more closely, that we had passed before, especially those that could be entered. With the light shining upon them, the crystallizations in one or two of those rooms were something brilliant and beautiful. After two hours of this exploration of the rooms, we went back to Uncle's, a somewhat tired crowd.

On the fourth day we renewed our journey; brother and his partner buying cattle where they found a cheap lot for sale, in Alabama, Mississippi, Tennessee and Kentucky, gathering about three hundred head.

We crossed the Mississippi at Mills Point, ferrying the cattle over, I suppose about forty at a load. Lewis and I went over with the first load, and Mat., remained to herd those left behind. After getting the first load off the boat, Lewis returned with the boat, and I herded those taken over.

It was seemingly almost human, the interest manifested on the part of those cattle to return to those left on the other side.

And at times it was quite a little trouble to keep some of them from taking the water in an effort to swim back.

While heading off some that were making for the river, a white dog came to my assistance, and soon put a stop to their efforts along this line.

Whether this dog had become lost from some former drover crossing there, we never knew, but he most persistently refused to be separated from us after that, and followed us the rest of the afternoon and remained over night when we ceased trying to scold him back. By accident, or otherwise, the majority of his caudal appendage had been amputated, so we named him Bob. Whether he had known the name formerly or not, he seemed to take a fancy to it, and Bob he was all the way to California, and quite a helpful Bob, too, on many occasions.

While driving in the Mississippi bottoms, which we did for some days, we were passing occasional farm houses and small lots of stock, hogs, cattle, etc.

A little after noon one day, we noticed a pig, weighing perhaps forty or fifty pounds, going along with the cattle, and I was deputized to drive it from among them. I did so and kept it to one side and held it back till the hindmost cattle had passed, when I took my place in driving the cattle. But in short order Mr. Pig was again seen with the drove. Again I was put in commission, and this time drove it back the road a hundred or more yards. But this young porker seemed to think he had as much right to take a journey as other cattle. No sooner would I cease my efforts to drive him back than he would renew his to return to the drove.

Finally I gave him a big boost toward his supposed home, and turned my horse and trotted briskly to the drove. It was not long till we discovered that piggy had played us the same trick the man did the fifty Indians, when fighting them single handed; he had surrounded us and was up near the front of the line. I tried the same game on him some more; but that pig sure must have thought he had been born somewhere out west, and wanted to get back home, for when we camped that night (we had a wagon and camping outfit now) he was promptly on hand, chirk and cheery as you please.

We wanted to leave him with the farmer where we camped and fed our cattle, but he said not so, as it was not his pig, and as he had so persistently stayed with us for half a day, we should just let him alone till he stopped of his own accord. He was up bright and fresh next morning and ready for an early start. As he had met with the same misfortune as our dog and, as we already had one Bob, we dubbed him stiff tail, and Stiff Tail he was to the end, later to be told. But I think that pig was a Missourian, for he was never satisfied till we made a halt in that state. Either that or he must have concluded he was a cow, for he stayed with them while he lived.

Mat., (whose parents, as before mentioned, were neighbors of my Father and were earnest, faithful Christians and members of the Baptist Church) had become an exceedingly profane man. In driving in the bottoms the undergrowth in places was quite thick, and cattle, especially when tired, seemed to know their advantage, and to take great pleasure in worrying their drivers, as the drivers sometimes did them.

Then it was that Mat. would unloose the latchet of his vocabulary of profanity, which seemed to be limitless, for he could run the entire gamut and never miss a note. But one day his horse, Crocket by name, was taken with the colic, I hardly think, though, from an overdose of chestnuts, and in a few hours was dead. He was a noble little animal and Mat. thought as much of him as a man well could of a horse. Anyhow for two weeks Mat. swore no more. Finally, though, the cattle became very troublesome, the brush was thick, and again he loosened up.

Being but a boy, I, though a church member, never felt it my prerogative to attempt to advise or offer counsel to men. On this occasion, however, I thought I'd risk it. So, after he had cooled down and everything was going smooth, I asked him how it was that, for two weeks, he had succeeded in refraining from swearing and had now turned loose again with even increased vigor. His reply was "I'll be d_____d if I know". Then I quit.

Brother and his partner decided to drive into winter quarters on Little Black River in Arkansas, which we reached somewhere about the 20th of October.

We crossed to the west side of this river at what was known as Asburry's Ford. It was a narrow stream, but deep with steep banks and with only occasional places at which it was fordable. Driving up the river about three miles, a place immediately on the banks of the stream was chosen as the location for our camp, after two or three days' inspection of the surrounding country. We were about forty miles south, or perhaps west of south slightly, from Poplar Bluffs, and our camp was built, as nearly as known, exactly on the line between Arkansas and Missouri. So we slept in one state and ate in the other, thinking a change of locality might be good.

The swamp was about forty miles wide, and the settlements were from three to twelve miles apart, with from four to five families in a settlement. Our nearest neighbors were the Asburry's, three miles south, while the next nearest were ten miles to the north.

The surface of the country was low and level, and covered with strips of fine large oak and hickory trees, then a slough, always emptying its waters from rains into Black River, thus draining the large extent of these low-lying lands. These sloughs were always lined on either side for the fourth mile, more or less, with large cypress trees, while the sloughs themselves were generally from eight to twelve yards wide, and thickly studded with cypress knees, a kind of stump looking growth from two to ten feet in height, always cone shaped and invariably hollow. Along these sloughs, more or less frequent in occurrence, were also cane-brakes, or patches of cane, varying in size from a small patch to several acres in extent.

These furnished the principal food during the winter for our stock, both horses and cattle. And they did quite well, feeding upon the leaves, which are ever green.

The fourth day after our arrival, Mat. took Lewis to the Mississippi River where he (Lewis) took boat for Saint Louis, Missouri, to arrange supplies for our trip across the plains. Wagons were to be built for the purpose, ox yokes, chains, etc., with tents, bedding and whatever was necessary. Having made the journey three times before, he well understood how to make all necessary arrangements for it.

I was left, of course, to look after camp affairs, with Bob for a companion, and a lonely time we two had for four days, the time Mat. was gone. At night, however, it was different. These swamps, or bottom lands (for they were not marshy) were infested with the large grey or timber wolves. They not only could, but did, make night hideous, to me, at least, with their howling. One could make seemingly as much, and as many different kinds of noise, as would a dozen dogs howling at the same time.

I was told to sleep in the wagon and to take Bob in with me. The cover to the wagon was made of good, strong sail canvas, and could be well fastened down at the sides with strong leather straps and buckles at the sides; and at the ends were large open seams, through which were put light strong cords and by these the ends of this cover could be drawn together, thus completely closing it, so that nothing could get out or in.

Well, you may be sure I made everything as secure as straps and cords could make them, and Bob and I turned in for the night, he lying close to my feet. I was just beginning to feel dozy when, in the distance, I heard, as it seemed to me, half a dozen different and most hideous noises at the same time, ending finally with one long, lonesome, doleful howl. Being the first of the kind I ever heard, I could not, of course, know what it was. But I was not left to guess a great while, for scarcely had the first ceased, before in another direction the first was repeated and then still another somewhere else, until it seemed the whole woods were filled with them. To make bad matters worse, for I assure you they were already bad enough, I found from all directions they seemed to be coming for the camp. I felt that I was in no danger as they could not get to me if they desired, and I had a good doublebarrelled shot gun, and both barrels loaded, besides Bob. But that dog made me more trouble than the wolves, for he seemed determined to get out, and have some sort of a mix up with them, for they were soon around the wagon. I felt certain that the mix would not be favorable to Bob, so, while I was quite sure he could not get out, to make assurance doubly sure, I took a small rope and tied it around his neck and tied each end to a bow of the wagon cover, thus securing him about midway of the wagon. The wolves not being satisfied with what they soon found was a failure, so far as the contents of the wagon were concerned began a fight among themselves.

Chapter III

Now, you may think I felt no interest in their amusement among themselves, but I did. For, first of all, there was no bone of contention among them, so far as I could see, and I was positive there was none from camp cooking, as we only had bacon in the wagon and there were no bones in it. But they fought just the same. And I am not able even at this late date to tell which was the more anxious to see that fight, the boy or the dog that was in the wagon. I talked to Bob and tried to persuade him to keep quiet, as it was not his fight, and he replied in his own way, but whether he was trying to persuade me to not peep under the edges of the wagon cover and look at what he was not permitted to see, I never could find out.

As to the outcome of that fight or its general order, if there was any order to it, I knew nothing, for I could see nothing. I felt very much, though, as the old lady expressed herself when she saw her husband and a bear fighting, and said she never saw a fight in her life in which she felt so little interest as to who won.

I suppose they got all they wanted of it, and perhaps some of them more, for they quit, whether they were satisfied, all hands around, with results or not. Anyhow, we in the wagon were glad when they left, at least, I was, and as I heard nothing to the contrary from Bob, I supposed he was also.

As nothing occurred to disturb us the remainder of the night, boy and dog alike, we slept quite soundly until morning.

About two hundred yards from our wagon was a log cabin, built by some parties who were getting out stave timber to ship to New Orleans the next spring. This was oak trees sawed into blocks six feet long and split into pieces of size and shape ready to be dressed into staves for making large tubs or barrels, etc.

These men's homes were on Crowley's Ridge about twenty miles East at the eastern edge of the swamp, and they were at their homes for some two weeks at this time. I took possession of that cabin next day, and had Bob and myself shut in and the wolves out when night came on, for they came earlier, were more numerous, stayed later and fought worse than the night before.

I suppose, though, they made final settlement of their troubles, or concluded the proceeds from camp supplies didn't pay for their serenade and tragical performance both, and the two seemed to go together. It may be they thought Bob and I were an unappreciative audience, or that we were too small a crowd for them to play to. At any rate, they came no more. I cannot say how Bob felt about it, as he failed to express himself in their absence, but was full of expression during the performance. As for myself, I enjoyed their absence very much indeed. Somehow, things seemed much more quiet, serene and orderly.

On the fourth day at evening Mat. returned, and we spent the night in the cabin, as he appeared to feel that intimate acquaintance with my visitors was not specially desirable to him any more than to myself.

This, his return, was on Friday. Saturday was spent looking among the cattle to see how they were doing. Sunday we rested, and Monday began the construction of our dwelling house for the winter. Particular description of our abode need not be given further than to say the walls were composed of cane, cut and carried on our shoulders a little less than a quarter of a mile, set on end, and leaned against poles placed in forked poles set in the ground. These poles for the cane to rest against were fourteen feet long on the sides, and ten at the ends; our building being ten by fourteen feet, seven of which were in Missouri and seven in Arkansas, or supposed to be, so that if it became unhealthy in one state, we could live entirely in the other by crowding a little, boarding in Missouri and sleeping in Arkansas.

The walls we made about eighteen inches thick for comfort and wolves' sake, etc. We then bound other poles midway the height of the walls, which held them securely in place, leaving a space for the door. The roof was covered with boards split from a cypress which we cut. And in this we fared sumptuously in the day and comfortably of a night upon a bed of small leafy cane, placed on a scaffold in one corner of our mansion.

I said we fared sumptuously, and so we did. We brought abundant supplies of flour, bacon and beans; and wild game, deer and turkey were plentiful all about us, and fine fish and turtle in the river at our feet. As to the turtle, thereby, not thereto, hangs a tale, not a tail. But this comes in later, not the tail, but the story.

I may profitably pass the entire winter, perhaps, by saying one day in general was as another. For we spent them looking after the stock, which soon became quite disposed to separate into small bands, and these in turn to scatter over too great an extent of country. So our time was occupied in looking after and keeping them from straying too far away.

Of course, we had sufficient time to attend to camp, to fish and kill all the game desired for camp purposes, and to enjoy ourselves generally, which we succeeded in doing quite beyond first expectations.

Unless the cattle were getting too much scattered, we looked after them on foot, walking miles every day, and in such case carried one, and sometimes two, guns, one each, as we had a shot gun and a rifle. Mat. always took one, though I did not.

Bob was a constant companion on these tramps, sometimes a helper in the way of game, and at others quite the opposite. Get a dog among a bunch of wild turkeys and they are almost sure to take to trees, and there is a chance to get a shot at one; they seem more intent on watching the dog than man. But it requires quite a sly hunter to slip upon them on the ground.

On one occasion, when we were out, Mat. had the shot gun (and this was before the day of cartridges) and before we saw them, or they us, we were in the midst of a bunch of three deer. The dog had them so excited that for a time they did not know just what to do, and circled about us several times quite close to us. Indeed, one ran so near me that I tried to catch it, of which I suppose I would have been more sorry than the deer, had I succeeded.

In the time Mat. was trying to shoot one, declaring that one of them stopped so near him he had scarcely room for the gun between him and the deer. He snapped both barrels in the time, under conditions in which he could not have failed to kill in either case. The deer, however, recovered from their confusion and escaped entirely unharmed.

Not so with Mat., though, as to his mental and moral state. He was mad all over because of the failure of his gun to fire, and gave it a round cursing, about which, so far as I could see, the gun was wholly unconcerned. He even threatened to bend it round a tree and still no concern on the gun's part. Before proceeding to draw the loads, as he concluded would be better than the bending process, he decided to try two more caps on it, and both barrels fired in fine order.

And then he was mad all through, but like the man going up hill with his cart full of loose apples, when he reached the top, found the tail board had fallen from his cart and the apples were scattered all the way up. When asked by a friend, who was passing, why he did not swear as usual, Mat. replied that he could not do the subject justice and it was no use. So Mat. said nothing, but putting his gun on his shoulder, we went straight to camp, although it was some time till night.

Chapter IV

We secured a rope and stretched it across the river just back of our camp, to which we attached a few fish hooks and thus secured all the fish we cared for. One morning Mat. went to see if we had a fish for breakfast. On taking hold of the first line, which could be reached from a narrow margin between bank and water, he found it seemingly hung on something, but pulling on the hook, which was quite a large one as much as he thought it, would bear, he found it would give to him. So he kept pulling until a turtle's head appeared, and finally its back, above the water. When it refused to come further. He called me. I went to his help. Getting a limb with a fork on it, I got a hold on the back part of his shell and, between the two of us, we managed to work his turtleship out on solid ground, and finally around in front of the camp. We held his head, which he constantly tried to draw into the shell, but would give way to the pain of the hook hung in his mouth, and I chopped its head off. It was a monster, at least to us, for neither of us had ever seen one near approximating it in size. When we had cleaned all the meat from the shell, the back or upper shell, if memory serves me right, measured twenty-two inches one way and twenty-four the other. This is the turtle with two—well one t-a-i-l and one t-a-l-e, one fastened to it and one just told.

In the spring when the mountain snow melts, Black River (this one called Little Black, as there are two of them) is not small by any means. When the snows are abundant in the mountains, the river backs its waters into all the sloughs, which are quite numerous on both sides of the river. Hence almost all that region of country is overflowed. There is no damage resulting, however, in that part, for as previously said, the land lies low. The River itself has but little fall, and the flood waters are all, or nearly all, back water with but little current.

The flood waters attain almost no depth, save in the sloughs, but the land is thoroughly saturated with water just at the surface, even where it is not on it. Hence, I suppose, the general name of the "Swamps of Black River" which at such times it well deserves.

The water at our camp became sufficiently warmed to be pleasant for bathing. One day I concluded to have a bath. I was no expert swimmer, but could paddle around fairly well.

After being in the water for a time, I concluded to swim across the river, which was, at this time, about thirty or forty yards in width. I swam across quite handily and climbed out on the bank. After sitting there for a time, I began to dread the return trip; in fact, became somewhat afraid to undertake it. I knew if I called for any one to bring the canoe over for me, the boys would laugh at me for being cowardly.

Of the two things, I dreaded more to be called a coward than to tackle the swim. So I plunged in and started out pretty well. But the further I went the more frightened I became, and soon found myself kicking and pawing for dear life. And kick and paw was all I was doing, excepting to drift down the current, for I was about half way across. Seeing my frantic efforts were accomplishing nothing but my exhaustion, I mentally said this, or felt it, if you chose to put it that way: "If I am going to drown, I'll do it just as easily as anybody on earth can." Immediately upon this conclusion, I started out and swam with as much or more ease to myself than ever, either before or since.

I really think this was the best lesson in the way of self control I ever had. For surely had I continued my useless exertions, I soon would have been exhausted and have drowned. Many persons lose their lives simply from want of self control. And not only in like circumstances, but under such as may be quite different.

But I was not the only one who had an experience in Black River. Mat. also on one occasion decided to have a bath. He could barely swim at all and getting beyond his depth, he had quite a struggle to get out. After dressing, he swore he was never going in water any more 'til he became an expert swimmer and, so far as I know, he never did.

The winter finally passed, as all winters have within my recollection; the grass sprang up in the bottoms, and being just enough in the beginning to make the stock anxious for it, but not enough to satisfy them, they began to ramble badly. Early and late, therefore and on horseback all the time, we had to go, and then found it almost impossible to keep them within bounds.

Lewis came down from Missouri and with him a young man who said his name was Dick but that they called him Richard for short. I failed to fall in with the fashion, however, and called him by his right name, Dick. This appeared to please him and he called me Joe in return. We soon became very good friends indeed.

We gathered the cattle as soon as we could, and on counting, found we were four short. Dick, Lewis and I started for Lafayette County, Missouri, where the outfit for the plains was to be shipped. Of course, we drove but few miles each day, as the cattle were thin and the grass of insufficient strength and quantity for them to bear any great distance per day. They must be allowed ample time to feed as well as rest. Several days were required to carry us out of the swamp.

Just here I am reminded that I owe Stiff Tail an apology, as he was an Arkansan instead of a Mississippian, for it was in the Black River, and not the Mississippi River, Bottoms, that he fell in love with us. It would never do to mix or misplace his pigship with any other stock or locality. In proof of which I offer the following fact, here for the first time made historical, in evidence.

After a few days' travel he became foot sore and leg weary, and I caught him and put him in the wagon, which I was driving them.

Of course, as any other intelligent swine would have done, he made somewhat strenuous objection, but climbing in with him and holding him until he became convinced what it all meant, he soon grew reconciled to his new experience as to the method of travel, laid himself down and rested contentedly. After a time he showed signs of having a desire to foot it again, and I put him out.

Ever after this, when he got tired, he would come up from the rear end of the cattle where he generally traveled and would come as near asking for a ride as any pig I ever ever listened to. And he always got it.

I don't think he understood the English language very well, for he did not speak it plainly, but he did as well as any Arkansas swamp pig could do, for the people in that part of the state had rather a peculiar way of expressing themselves. Indeed, I had an idea that most of them were refugees from justice, as they generally appeared to be on the lookout for something. Otherwise, they were as thoroughly contented as any people I have ever been with.

They had nothing, not even a title to their homes, as the land at that time had not been placed on the market by the Government. Neither did they seem to want more than they had, although it was the best place to make quick and easy money I have ever seen.

Outsiders would come in, and bring men with them (for the natives could not be hired to work at any price) and cut logs of cypress sixty feet long, averaging three feet in diameter in their length, raft them to New Orleans, the entire cost being five dollars per log (called a tier) and as we were told, sell them there for fifty dollars per tier.

Chapter V

When the swamp citizens wanted any "stoe goods" as they called them, they took their collections of deer, coon, muskrat, and whatever other kinds of skins they had on hand to the store, and traded them for such merchandise as they might need.

We arrived at our point of destination in due time, and found that our outfit from St. Louis had not come. Nor did it in time for us to cross the plains that year, 1855, so we were detained in Missouri for a year, and that is how we came to be Missourians.

Well, we were none of us ashamed of our *nativity by adoption,* for we found Missourians to be as nice, social, open and kind-hearted people as could be desired, current rumor other places to the contrary, notwithstanding.

Finding that we could not get off on our journey that year, Mat. and Lewis secured from Mr. Bledsoe, Dick's father a large tract of prairie land that had never been cultivated, and had the use of it that year for breaking it.

They rigged up two ox teams, four yoke to the team, and with two eighteen inch prairie plows, proceeded to plow it. My part of the contract was to drop corn in every alternate furrow, the sod from the next furrow covering it. That was all we ever did to it, and had a fine crop too. Such was the nature of the prairie sod that it must have a year in which to rot before it could be cultivated.

That fall, we cut the stalks with the corn on them, shocked them in the field, and thus had an abundance of feed to carry our stock through the winter in fine condition, although the winter was a very severe one according to general opinion of the citizens.

During the spring and summer and into the fall until snow began to fall, cattle did well on the grass, which grew so abundantly that many people cut their hay in the open prairie, and good hay it was. We put up enough for our horses, and with the corn they went through the winter fat and fine.

During the season, when not engaged with our corn crop, I worked for the farmers, plowing, harvesting, hauling rails, etc., and made me quite a little money', which I invested in yearling calves, to drive across to California and thus secure my fortune and return to my native state. Three years was the time I gave myself to get rich and get back home. As to the time, I missed my calculations only a little over half a century, it being fifty-three years before I set foot again on dear old South Carolina soil.

As to the fortune, I missed that even further than my guess on the time. For when I left my Father's home, I had ten cents in my pocket. And today I did have a nickel, but having a hole in the same pocket with the nickel I lost it. The hole was not in the same pants' pocket, however, that contained the dime. I thought it best to mention this, lest some should think I was trying to make the impression I was still wearing the same pants, but I am not. I am neither wearing the same pants, nor trying to make any impression of great importance.

Winter in Missouri was a time for general jollification, visiting, social parties, sleigh riding, and pleasant times generally. In the section where we were there were a large number of young people, boys and girls, from eighteen to twenty-five years old. All fine, gentlemanly and ladylike folks.

This was in Texas Prairie, twelve miles from South Wellington, a town on the Missouri River, and twenty miles southwest from Lexington, where Pap Price fought his celebrated battle behind his moving Hemp-ball fortification.

While this was four years before our family unpleasantness,[1] even then things were warming up some, out of, as well as in, Congress. This was specially true as between the "Red Legs" and "Border Ruffians". All one had to do to make a Missourian red hot, at least he would get red in the face and look hot, was to speak of the Kansans interfering with the Missouri "Niggers". Well, that's not only dead, but I understand that the last bit of wool, in the teeth or out of them, was buried too deep for resurrection in the great commemorative meeting of the Blue and the Gray on the memorable field of Gettysburg, this summer just past. So let us all bid it God speed into the vigorous of everlasting forgetfulness.

Missourians, as before stated, are a friendly, sociable, kind-hearted people as one could wish to know, but they had a thoroughly established opinion that they knew their rights, and were ready to maintain them at fisticuffs or otherwise.

There was a little town out of my neighborhood I am glad to say, generally known as "Lick-skillet" or the "Devil's Half Acre" more commonly the latter, where a certain class of them usually met on Saturdays to drink whiskey, fight out their old difficulties and differences, and create new ones for future reference of like character. I never was at the place, not wishing to be on intimate terms with the owner or his visitors but if reports were true, if his Satanic Majesty did not hold a quit claim deed to it, he certainly

---

[1] In "family unpleasantness" he is referring to the Civil War

held a heavy first claim mortgage, at an excessively high rate of interest on it.

When winter began, which was quite early that year, it started in for first class business in its line and maintained the high standard of its stock until late spring. The first snow was about eighteen inches in depth, and about the time it began to give promise of settling down into a good degree of firmness, another of almost equal quantity came down on top of it, though, of course, no one expected it to come on the bottom.

Semi-occasionally and sometimes oftener, this was repeated through the winter, and there was on the general level, two or more feet of snow for at least three months continuously. It was well frozen, so that sleighing was fine, but hard on stock. I saw many cattle that had pulled the bush of their tails off, where it had frozen fast in the ice or frozen snow during the night while they were lying down.

While this was the general level, in many places it had drifted badly, and but few fences were to be seen, as they were covered by the drifting snow. We hauled our stock feed on a long sled we made for the purpose, and I drove two and three yoke of oxen for weeks in succession over fences six and seven rails in height.

But spring came, though a little behind hand as to time; and then we were busy with final preparations for the long anticipated and, to me, anxiously looked forward to, start for California.

We had, however, to wait on the grass to gain sufficient strength to sustain the stock when traveling.

Chapter VI

Ho for California! For sure enough we were finally started but we were among the very latest for, as stated in the previous chapter, we were waiting for the grass to get enough strength to keep our cattle from running down in flesh on the start.

This being my brother's fourth time to cross with ox wagons, he knew the results of getting stock thus run down in the beginning. Many who were in a great hurry to get an early start that year found to their sorrow their mistake. The grass, young, washy and not very plentiful, stock gains but little, if any, strength from, and being unused to travel, fall off rapidly. You may be sure they have but small chance of gaining in flesh on the journey. It proves a great loss, rather than gain, as to time in the outcome. But the stories of people becoming snow bound in the Sierra Nevada Mountains made those unacquainted with the conditions anxious to get through early. Hence the great desire for an early start.

It was the seventh day of May, 1856. We bade our many Missouri friends goodbye and drove about five miles the first day. Made our camp about 2:00 P.M. after a late start in the morning and a long nooning. We increased a mile or two each day for the first three or four days, thus giving our stock ample time to feed, and also preventing them from becoming tired and sore from travel, stopping early in the afternoon, also giving them an opportunity to fill themselves before night, by reason of which they were more quiet during the night and were well rested by morning. It was slow moving in the start, but proved the wisdom of the course in the outcome. Starting about the last of the emigration, we reached the end of our journey far ahead of the middle of it.

In about six days, according to appointment, we joined forces with the Dickenson and Porter train, thus forming quite a strong combination for protection against any attack that might be made upon the train by Indians.

Our portion of the train consisted of seven men and one woman, as brother married the third day before we started. The Dickenson and Porter part proper had eight men and one woman, as Mr. Robert Dickenson also married a few days before starting. Then there was a Mr. Harris, who was bringing his mother and two sisters to California, who had his own outfit, and wagon and ten oxen; also a young man, Jamison, by name, with them. There also were three Acree brothers who had their own wagon and team. We, of course, formed but the one train, but the separate parties, as named, messed to themselves, that is, cooked and ate separately. Thus we were, counting all, twenty men and five women strong, and felt pretty well able to protect ourselves, as all were well-armed with guns and pistols.

We came together in the forenoon, camped early in the afternoon, and Lewis, Mat., the two Dickenson and the two Porter brothers, Mr. Harris, and the oldest of the Acree brothers, held a council of order for the remaining part of the way. The order of travel was as follows: the wagon taking the lead one day would take the rear the next. Thus alternating, gave each one his share of the dust, as it ordinarily became more dense toward the last or hindmost wagon, of which there were six; with from two to three yoke each. Hence there was no favoritism and no strife or contention.

There were now about five hundred head of cattle, and they decided to set a guard over them each night, not that there was yet any danger from Indians, but it would keep them together during the night, and they would not get far from camp while feeding after daylight, before starting time.

The guard was divided into two watches, two from dark until midnight and two from then until morning. It was the business of the guard to rouse the camp at daylight, so there could be an early start. Squads were appointed to take turns in collecting the stock after breakfast, while the rest prepared for starting. In the evening when we stopped, all hands proceeded to pitch camp, get wood and water, and make all necessary preparations for the night. My part of this work was to milk two cows. We had plenty of milk and butter all the way.

The butter making process was something new to most of us. The milk was strained into a large can made for the purpose, and the shaking of the wagon during the day became both separator and churn. Every evening there was a nice little batch of butter taken from the can, with the milk left for drinking.

You know it is said that "Necessity is the mother of invention". I have often wondered if this necessity may not have led to the present creamery system. I was also one of the teamsters for one of our wagons. Lewis drove the cook wagon in which his wife rode, and Bob Pool and I took turns of a half day each driving wagon and loose cattle. I drove the team forenoon and he after; about one-third of the way, when I was put in charge for full time. In that way it came about that I had the pleasure, if such you'd call it, of walking about three-fourths of the way from Missouri to California, for no teamster was allowed to ride in the wagon or on the tongue. The latter was dangerous and the former left your wheel oxen to pull most of the load, as one could not use his whip in the wagon because of the cover, and the part of the team in front of the wheelers soon learned they were out of danger and took advantage of it too. So walk I had to.

Those driving the loose stock each was assigned his position to be kept the journey through, two in the rear and three on either side of the drove. This kept the cattle from trying to feed off on either side, as they were inclined to do.

After the first two weeks, they took their places in the drove almost as regularly as did the drivers theirs. Certain ones were always at the hindmost part, and others choosing sides of the road on which they preferred to travel, while a certain long-bodied, long-legged cow with an amputated caudal appendage, without failure was ready to take her position immediately behind the last wagon, kept close up to it and, so far as I remember, I never saw her leave the road during the hours of travel. She formed the apex of the drove, or would, if it could have been stood upon its behindermost end.

Chapter VII

Another rule to be observed was that we were to stop two half days in each week, when good feed, wood and water could be had, on Sundays and Thursdays when these necessities could be had at such times. When they could not, we stopped the first such place we came to for a whole day. This, however, involved staying in the same place thirty-six hours, two nights and a day, which was objectionable for two reasons: it was difficult to find a place where feed, at a reasonable distance from camp for so many cattle could be found for that length of time. Within so lengthy a stop they would become more or less sore and stiff and would not travel so well for a time, while an over-night stop made no perceptible difference with them.

Generally, about three P.M. each day, Lewis and Mr. Robert Dickenson would ride ahead of the train to look out for a good camping place. It was the purpose to make about twenty miles per day; some times, however, owing to the needed supplies for camping, we had to go further and at others stop about half that distance.

These were the general rules governing us all the way. They proved to be excellent rules, as our stock did well, we made good time and had a good time generally all the way across. There were not to exceed half a dozen cattle lost in any way during the entire journey. One of these I may tell of, if I happen to think of it in the right place, as I was mixed up with it and thought at one time I was going to get badly mixed with something else.

Having said enough about the rules and regulations of the trip, I may now say something of some of the incidents of our journey, for they were altogether too numerous, and many of too little importance to admit of relating.

We were on the south side of Platte River, at our starting point. After some two or three weeks' traveling, we reached that stream. We traveled up the river for two or more weeks with nothing worthy of note, except one peculiarity which continued clear to the summit of the Rocky Mountains. It was this: Looking ahead one could see what appeared to be the summit of a ridge, apparently three or four miles distant, which gave the impression that, when reached, one could see any given distance beyond, if one's sight could reach that far, for there was nothing in sight beyond it. One peculiarity was, it was from five to ten, or any other number of times farther away than you thought it was, for you never reached it, which was another peculiarity. When you finally did get to where you thought it should be, it had either flattened out, moved on ahead–for there was another before you just like it–or otherwise disappeared. I inquired of several of the boys if they could tell me what became of those ridges. They said they could not, but denied most positively that they had taken any of them.

This might have made me somewhat suspicious, had I not thought from the appearance of their size–though that, like the ridge itself, might have been deceptive–they looking anywhere from ten to twenty miles in length–that they were rather large for private appropriation, without public notice, particularly under the then condition of things.

How that singular and deceptive appearance is produced, I have never been able to learn. It is not mirage, for it was a continuous thing. You could see it all day and day after day for weeks in succession.

There are a few general things I wish to speak of. There is an enlarged impression of bigness one gets in making that journey, as we made it and others in those days. Bigness of country, of the earth itself, and of things in general. As to impression of one's own largeness, it is much like the Chinaman's promotion in school. He said the professor promoted him backward. One feels as if his enlargedness was increasingly smaller, and that he might be expanded by a great many times his present dimensions without crowding things to any noticeable extent. I think I have seen a great many persons, men of large intelligence in a way, college graduates of high degree, that it would do a whole world of good to make that trip in that way. They manifest a feeling that they fill all the vacant space that can possibly be allowed for one person, and still are badly crowded. Crossing the plains with an ox wagon, and putting in six months of it, would either lead them to conclude there was an abundance of room for several persons of their own mammoth proportions, without disturbing the earth's equilibrium, or crowding any one off it. This impression can be either mental or physical, or both and should prove quite helpful in either or both cases. And if they were not benefited along the line of their particular ailment, it would certainly be because theirs was a hopeless case and they were richly deserving the sympathy of the rest of humanity, inmates of asylums and all.

The greatness of extent, the grandeur of, the apparent everlasting firmness and fixedness, the grand mountains in the distance, pile upon pile, away and away, seemingly limitless, the very mightiness of all. It is inspiring to personal smallness. And yet the invigorating atmosphere, the gentle brilliance of the light inspires to a desire for growth in true greatness; to be a coiner into words, actions and life, of something like the splendor of the scene that lies before one and the feelings that stir your deepest depths.

Many a day, boy that I was, I have driven my team along the road, with an inexpressible desire to flee to the great fountain of all knowledge and wisdom, and learn and learn and from and grow, forever and ever; at least, until I could know and be something that was worth being and knowing.

Speaking of the atmosphere, its clearness is something wonderful. Anything like guessing distance correctly is, to the uninitiated, an out and out impossibility. I had always felt pride in being a good judge of distance. One day a large rock came into view, standing squarely up above the ground, known as Court House Rock, which I thought I could have thrown a finger stone to at half a dozen throws at most. Brother asked me how far I thought it was to it. Having learned a little–just a little–of the deceptiveness of appearances in this respect, I thought I would rather over than under judge the distance and I said a mile. He said that on a former occasion he and others had ridden out to have a look at it. As near as they could judge by the speed traveled and the time occupied, it was twelve miles.

Chapter VIII

On passing old Fort Kearney, a short distance to the south of the road, we were reminded quite forcibly that we were getting into the Indian country, though we had seen but few. To dismiss the Indians in general I may say there was almost no trouble from them that year, while the preceding year and that following, fifty-five and fifty-seven, they were very troublesome. Many old plains men, however, assert that most difficulties were brought on or led by the Whites. Sometimes a young sprout of a smart Aleck, full of senseless deviltry, would conclude to show his wonderful courage, and would kill an unoffending, unarmed and helpless old squaw or buck, for which possibly half a dozen trains would have to suffer and lives; more or less, be lost, though I am happy to say nothing like this occurred in our train. Most of the trouble came about from Indians led by White—well, White devils, instead of red, on robbery intent. This was quite commonly charged to Mormons, and perhaps their morals were not wholly above suspicion.

There came to our camp, as it was getting dusky one evening, an Indian well dressed in white men's wear, carrying a fine blanket of their own make and a nice, large bed quilt. We suspected him to be a spy, and decided to place him under guard for the night. He was given to understand that, should he try to leave camp before morning, he would be shot. One of the boys, thinking that some kind of a brogue would make it plainer, raising his arms as if firing, said "Ve bang mit a gun". While the rest of us laughed heartily at this, the Indian smiled broadly and replied: "Yes, Ingin know."

After this all doubt as to one's being understood was settled by "Yes, Ingin know."

Mr. James Porter, a Methodist minister, sympathizing with the Indian, undoubled his large saddle blanket and spread it on the ground for the Indian to sleep on, leaving the blanket and quilt for him to cover himself with. In the early morning, while the guard was awakening the camp, which required by a minute or so, Mr. Indian made his escape accompanied by the preacher's blanket, much to the parson's disgust.

A few evenings later, as we were eating supper, there came another but minus everything but a scant breech cloth and, as we discovered on testing him, an immense extent of emptiness. He looked so longingly on while we were eating, that the sympathetic women undertook to fill him. But after all the leavings of rice, beans, meat, bread, etc., of our mess was successfully stored away, the hungry look still remaining, the others came to their relief. But all in vain, for after the entire camp was cleaned up, there was still a "more, please" look in the eye, that still showed a "void" in the stomach, whether it was an "aching" one or not. Some of the boys suggested that he be fed a log chain by way of dessert and extra filling.

Others thought the experiment unsafe, because in case of a possible explosion during the night, no one could say where the chain might strike.

He stayed all night with us under the loving watch care of a man with a gun, the soft warm earth for a bed and the canopy of the heavens for covering, as there were no more saddle blankets to spare. He seemed in no hurry to leave us, waiting very patiently for breakfast, which was given him in large quantity again, and we saw no more of him 'til supper was ready the next evening. He had managed to keep out of sight during the day, and the process was repeated the next day, and finding his food depository altogether too capacious to prove wholly financially satisfactory under the circumstances, he was dismissed and bidden a hearty welcome to make himself conspicuous by reason of permanent absence.

We kept along the main Platter to the junction of the North and south forks of the river, and up the south fork about twelve miles and camped, though it was yet quite early for camping. But Lewis and Mr. Dickenson,–and when I say Mr. for either of them, I mean Bob and not Abe, as Bob had a wife, but Abe didn't–rode down to the river and down the steep bank into the water and across it; here some half or three-quarters of a mile wide. Their purpose was to select a ford, which they had no trouble in doing. All hands, as far as tools could be supplied, and each wagon carried a shovel and pick, then went to work digging or cutting a passway down the bank for the wagons, which was soon done, the men taking turns at the work. Everything was then ready for crossing the river in the morning.

The Platte is a peculiar stream, at least 'til you get well up the Rocky Mountains, wide, shallow, sandy bottom, swift current, and not a drop of clear water in it that any one has discovered.

Next day under the circumstances, it was unfortunately my day to lead. However, with Lewis on horseback in front to guide me, with an assistant driver I drove in. Each team required two drivers, one on each side, as the constant tendency of the team was to drift down with the current by reason of its force. The depths nowhere reached to the beds of our wagons. But to prevent its doing so, constant movement was necessary, as the current was constantly washing the sand from under the wheels, a very short stop would cause the wagon to settle until the water would have been in the bed.

Even with continuous going, the sand was moved fast enough that the jolting of the wagon was as if driven over very stony ground.

We then drove across a roadless country for twelve miles to the emigrant road on the south side of North Platte.

I am not sure of the location of the following, as I am writing all of this from a memory which has been in service now for fifty seven years, and is becoming threadbare in spots. I think, however, it was on the north fork that one morning, just before breaking camp, Lewis called our attention to what looked like the stem of a tall chimney with the building gone, which he said was called Chimney Rock. It appeared to be ten or twelve miles away.

Now, to make a long story short, that is, to tell in a few moments what it took us three days to discover practically, we, traveling at the rate of twenty miles a day, camped at the end of the third day, opposite Chimney Rock. And this is that other illustration of the deceptiveness of appearance as to distance on the plains, before spoken of. But don't get in a hurry over this thing, for we are not yet done with it, as the following proves.

After camp work was done, several of the boys started out to get a close view of it and to carve their names in the rock which was said to be quite soft, to give notice to Indians and others of equal prominence in that part of the national possession, that they had been there and had thus immortalized themselves.

The sun was about two hours high when the boys started, promising themselves a tramp of a half or three-quarters of a mile and return.

As usual the cooks prepared, and the rest of us ate supper before dark, minus the ambitious part of the camp. About half past eight, we at camp began feeling somewhat uneasy lest they might have been picked up by some roving band of Indians, or that they were lost.

So we began making arrangements to look after them. Horses were brought in and saddled and, as it was one of the rules that a gun was never to be fired after night only under pressing necessity, it was agreed that, in case the searching party should not find them in half an hour, that a single shot should be fired at camp and every fifteen minutes after that the searchers might be kept in touch, as it were, with its location.

Just as all arrangements were completed, however, we heard "Halloo" a short distance away.

When they arrived, of course, everybody wanted to know about Chimney Rock. And after close enough questioning, they finally confessed that it looked just as far off at dark, or near dark, as it did when they started from camp. So they concluded their enterprise with a cold supper, a la buck Indian and as for immortality it was postponed for future reference.

Chapter IX

Occasionally, and sometimes lasting a mile or more, on the banks of the rivers, and particularly on the Humboldt, there were dense willow growths, quite close to which the road sometimes ran. Frequently during quite long drives by these, anything else would be suggested as readily as Indians.

After the last persons of the train had passed and no great distance either, on looking back, the edge of the willows would look quite thick with them. It was ever the purpose of those selecting camping places to choose them well away from the willows. It gave the Indians too good a chance, should they desire, which they frequently did in other years, to shoot from their hiding, either man or beast. This they could do in the dark with no suspicion of any harm being done, should they make a killing shot, as bow and arrow makes no report.

The cattle, after feeding in the evening until time to collect them, were generally gathered near the wagons, and would soon lie down and rest quietly until near midnight, when they would get up and want to feed. But holding them well within bounds for an hour or so, they soon lay down again and would rest until about day light. Our chief effort was to keep them a good bow shot away from the willows. This meant greater safety for the guards also.

On gathering the drove one morning, one of our main work oxen was found missing. On searching out the willow patch, which fortunately on that occasion was small, it was found that, escaping the notice of the guard, he had somehow gotten into the willows and came out on the opposite side, and had either strayed or was driven away. Mr. Birdwell and myself were sent to find him, while the train moved on, as there were others that could be put in his place.

We found him some miles from where we had camped and got back near our camping place of the previous night when, night coming on and we being tired, as also were our horses, we found a good place and stopped for the night. Tying the ox and our horses in a small hollow or low place, we, though quite hungry, made pillows of our saddles, covering with our saddle blankets and slept very well 'til morning. On awaking, we found our ox had broken his rope and was gone again.

We searched for him 'til about 10 o'clock and gave him up, as his tracks led us away from the road and in an almost straight line. We concluded he was being driven and not caring to take any chances on our own safety further, we started to overtake the train. We did not go directly to the road, but rode in an oblique direction toward it. In an hour or two we got to where we could see the dust rising from the trains on the road.

Looking ahead and to our left, we saw a number of persons on horseback quite a distance from us, riding rapidly. We watched them for a few minutes and concluded they were coming toward us and, keeping our respective rates of speed and directions, could easily come between us and the road, and that they were Indians trying to cut us off from the road. Changing our direction more immediately for the road, we also put our horses to the gallop, and decided to give them the best race for it that we could. We soon saw that they had increased their speed. I suppose they saw we did the same, or could, had they been close observers, for we were in just as much of a hurry as they were. I suppose the race lasted four or five miles, and the further, the faster, or harder anyway, for we soon had our travel-tired horses at full speed. Well, it was who should and who shouldn't, and we fully decided we should if we could. Making what we felt was our final dash, we came within a mile or so of the road with a large train ahead of us.

Seeing they could not make it, as we supposed, anyway, they veered to their right quite sharply and left us. Seeing this, we were not in so great a hurry and came quickly to a walk to give our horses a breathing spell, of which they were sadly in need.

Of course, we were not afraid at all, but having no desire to form intimate acquaintance with Indians in whom we had no special interest, only to keep well away from, we did urge our horses considerably to this end.

We came to the road and found the train to be that of a Mr. Phillips, of which more anon and perhaps of more interest that this episode. This was the one particular occasion of the trip that I feared I was liable to get more than I had called for.

We overtook our train about 2 P.M., two hungry and tired boys, as we had been riding constantly in daylight without anything to eat since breakfast the day before. This ox was the only animal of the bovine order lost from our division of the train during the trip.

A young man in our mess, Bob Clarkson, was perhaps twenty-one or twenty-two years old, and myself were the youngest in the train, being myself then in my sixteenth year.

It was about the big sleepytime of boyhood with us and losing two half nights on guard each week, and the plains being the greatest place of all to sleep anyway, it was quite hard to wake us up of a morning. The boys said they would call and we answer, but speaking for myself, I always got up when I was wakened enough to know what I was doing.

I suspect the boys thought it was a case of "a little more sleep, and a little more slumber, and a little more folding of the arms for slumber" and thought they would try the effects of cold water for an awakener.

Well, it had the desired effect and then some, at least with Clarkson. We were both professors of religion, but somehow his did not seem to be of the staying kind. Like the fellow who, when asked if he was sanctified, replied: "Yes, in spots." Bob's profession might have been somewhat spotted at the start, and the spots were pretty well gone already. At any rate, he could swear with most any of them and was up and out of the tent and wanting to fight anybody, particularly those who threw the water. But no one seemed in a fighting humor at the time, but quite the contrary; they were having their own fun with him. Thinking if they did that way with him, man as he was, although the application moved one quite suddenly, I concluded, being only a boy, it would be foolish for me to manifest any temper in the matter, so I joined as heartily in the laugh as any one, even if I did have to force it a bit.

Chapter X

Having found the water to be very effective, particularly in arousing Bob's ire, if nothing else, they continued to apply it with uncomfortable regularity, until the head waters of the Humboldt were reached, when one morning, the covering was quietly taken from over us and almost a full bucket was thrown on each of us.

Well, of course, Bob was good and mad, as well as wet, and was dressed and out of the tent hunting a fight before I began dressing. While very wet, I was not mad until I reached down for my pants, I suppose my cold, wet clothing must have struck my get-mad-quick spot. For I was mad, and mad before I had time to think. Securing dry clothing, I dressed and went out, but had fully decided to say nothing, also I didn't want any one to say anything to me. But they did, thinking to have some fun at my expense also. I think, however, they were disappointed, for without showing any signs of anger, at least trying not to, I very quietly, but seriously, promised them that—well, I won't say just what I did promise, as I have been ashamed of it myself for fifty years. Possibly they were also; anyhow, I had no more water thrown on me afterward. But I learned this lesson: when a human being, through anger, loses what little sense he may have, he is about the biggest fool of any animal that lives. He is not himself nor anything else that I have knowledge of but a fool, even a poor specimen of that. I was never mad before, have never been since, and my earnest desire and devout prayer is that I may never be again.

This puts me somewhat ahead of my story, so I must go back a few hundred miles to the Platte again, as there are two or three Indian stories to be told yet.

Driving alone one day, we met a mounted band of fifteen or twenty Indians, all painted. Whether it was war paint or fancy dress for a dance or party of some kind, none of us were sufficiently posted as to their customs to know. They were perfectly quiet until they had passed the leaders of the loose cattle, when setting up a sort of half yell and half cackle, they started on a gallop and immediately the cattle, on the run also, turned to follow them. Almost before one could think, the whole drove was so much excited it required the best efforts of the drivers to prevent a bad stampede. What the purpose of the Indians was, unless it was to stampede them, we could not know, and they certainly did not stop to explain.

There is something remarkable about how a band of long traveled, worn down and tired cattle will, without almost any cause apparently, become instantaneously frenzied, seemingly from fright. When the fright is sufficiently great, they are entirely unmanageable. This is what cattle men call a stampede.

On one evening no camping place and feed could be found close together. There was an open island formed by a slough or channel cut by the river, on which was fine feed. The camp was pitched about a quarter of a mile from the island, which was about a mile in length. The stock was driven on the island and the guard set as usual. Between two and three o'clock in the morning, as the guard stated, everything was just as quiet as could be apparently, but instantly every animal in the drove was on foot and going pell mell for the further end of the island.

There were several bells among the cattle, and knowing by these rattling and the sound of the running stock that something was wrong, all hands that could be spared from camp were at once out and after them. They were finally quieted down without getting off the island. There was no more sleeping, however, that night. We could not discover what gave them their fright, but concluded that it was either an Indian trying to stampede them or a Coyote had gotten among them.

Our way lay on the south side of the North Platte, from twelve miles above the junction of the two rivers to within about forty miles of the north crossing of that fork. That point, so far as I know, had no name, although Uncle Sam had some soldiers there at the time, their occupancy was but temporary although they had a small fort made of logs, but where they came from was a mystery, as there was not a tree in sight. They were expecting a band of warriors, a thousand strong, that day or the next.

Whether they were coming for treaty or fighting purposes, the soldiers did not know and we never learned. They tried to persuade our leaders to await their coming, as they said it would be wholly unsafe for us in case they were on the war path.

But our people in council decided we would move on and take the chances. And we were fortunate enough to see nothing of them.

There was a bridge across the river here, kept by a man who had a trading post also, with supplies for emigrants. The price for crossing on the bridge was twenty-five cents per head for cattle and two dollars and fifty cents for wagons. The stream here was about one hundred feet wide, but deep, so it was not fordable for wagons. So all the cattle were unloosed from the wagons and unyoked, except the wheel yokes and swam across with the loose cattle. Then the wagons were driven over on the bridge pulled by the wheelers alone.

Near this point we left the Platte for good, and traveled across the country to Green River. Here a method novel to the most of us was adopted to get our wagons across the river without getting the stuff wet, as the water was deep enough to come well up into the beds, and none of them was water tight.

There being quite a growth of timber here, there was no difficulty in finding a small tree, which was soon chopped down and several blocks fourteen inches in length cut off and split into smaller pieces, two dozen of which were required. Then raising the wagon boxes, one of these pieces was tied to each standard and the boxes let down on them, leaving a couple of inches of the standards to hold them. In this way they were raised just above the water and went over dry. We had no cause for repeating this on any other part of the way.

In a few days we came near to the summit of the Rocky Mountains. In passing over this there was a long cañon, through which was a smooth, but in some cases quite a steep road. It was a hard day's drive through it.

Hence it was the aim of those who understood to camp as close to the cañon's mouth or entrance as feed could be found. It had been eaten off back three or four miles perhaps, when we arrived. We made an early start next morning and by noon reached the summit. Off to our left a few yards was a large, nice spring of good water, and we nooned there.

Chapter XI

Resting our stock here and eating lunch, after an hour, we started on the descending slope of the Rockies, which as our road ran, we found to be much more abrupt than the ascent, for it was up, up, up, and seemingly up without end. Unless, though, one noticed the current of the river, which always and everywhere was quite swift, the ascent mostly was barely perceptible. But if one looked back, he could see plainly the fall in the land, and the ever recurring ridges referred to before us showed distinctly its rising character. For hundreds of miles this was true, with only an occasional, more abrupt rise to break the monotony. And having attained an elevation, it was very rarely, if ever, that a descent of any consequence was made, until the final start from the summit.

This spring, if not the real head of the Humboldt River, was at least the first we saw whose waters empty into the Pacific Ocean finally, for it flows west and becomes part of that river at any rate, and has its rise immediately on the summit of the mountains.

We reached the western end of cañon with the sun about one hour high, which was later than our usual time to drive. The grass here, as at the eastern end, was well eaten off by those before us for quite a distance. Our camp hunters, however, had found good grass nearly a mile to the right and around the point of a mountain. So they decided to camp at the cañon's mouth and drive the cattle to the feed, that being nearer than any to be had on the road. Driving them around, all but two of the men returned to camp and ate supper, and a triple guard then went out, three for the fore, and three for the latter, part of the night, as it was always well to be cautious. The wisdom of the course was well proven in this instance.

That evening, as it was getting dark, two men rode up to the camp and, speaking to my brother, said they, with another man, had started from Oregon on horseback to return to the east, with pack animals carrying their outfit. In crossing some river, the name of which I have forgotten, as he told the story, swollen by recent rains, their partner was drowned and their pack horses and provisions lost also. There being a very light emigration on that road, and a poor chance to get anything to eat, they turned across to the California road. The spokesman talked very much as one whose voice was weak from hunger. He said they had had nothing to eat for three days and wanted to buy some food. Brother told him we had nothing to spare in the provision line but, under the circumstances, would have some supper fixed.

But he objected to this, saying they had a camp a mile or two further down and wanted to pay for what they got, as they had not lost their money. Lewis sold them, I think it was, two dollars worth of bacon and beans, some crackers and a little flour. The man handed him a five dollar piece and received his change and they rode away. By some means Lewis failed to put the coin in his purse dropping it into his pocket.

All was a stir at an early hour next morning and those at camp having eaten breakfast, went to gather and drive in the cattle, while the guard came in and ate their breakfast. The order of the day was we would stop at the first good feed and watering place and lie over for the remainder of the day. In the meantime,

Lewis putting his hand in his pocket, felt the coin and took it out to put into his purse.

In daylight it proved an easily detected counterfeit. Whereupon he, Mat. and Bob and Abe Dickenson took their pistols, mounted their horses and rode to where the men said they were camped. There, instead of two, they found five men in bed. With arms ready for immediate use, if necessary, Lewis told his man the money received from him was counterfeit and he wanted good money, both for the provisions sold and the change given him. He, of course, expressed great surprise as well as readiness to make good. He said it had been given him in change before leaving the Oregon road. Turning to one of his bedfellows, who kept their positions in bed, he borrowed a twenty-five dollar piece of the same coin, and offered that in making good. Of course, it would have done so for himself, in case he had gotten good money in change again. Upon seeing this, each of our men drew and presented his pistol, and Lewis told them every one to remain motionless while this fellow should immediately pay him in full.

Without further ado, he did so. Our men then rode away, keeping their back eye well open until beyond range of pistol shot.

We drove about five or six miles and, finding feed, etc., camped for the day and night, to give the stock a good rest, as they had been on the go for a week then without it.

That afternoon a man came from the Philips train, then camped at the eastern end of the cañon, asking for help, stating that about twenty head of their cattle had been stolen the night before and they had trailed them well up into the mountains toward the west. Knowing nothing of the number concerned in the theft, they had not a force of their own that was strong enough to risk following them further, and so were seeking help. A couple of trains being in sight ahead and resting as were we, the rider went to them and got two from each. Two of us went with them and three of their own, left up the cañon a short distance to watch, made ten in the company.

We rode up the cañon intending, when opposite the point to which they had followed the trail, to leave the road and reaching that point to follow it until they were overtaken, which those who had followed it that far, thought we would be no great while in doing, as the tracks were quite fresh where they left them.

On coming near the spring at the summit, a smoke was seen rising at the spring. The leader had the rest stop while, leaving his horse, he investigated. In a few minutes he returned saying there were five in number and the cattle there resting, having probably been driven rapidly after getting them away from camp.

There being quite a growth of timber and underbrush and those at the spring having a good time, judging from the noise made, we were upon them before they discovered us, every man ready for battle if needful. They were so taken by surprise, and as we discovered, their firearms were with their saddles, they made no effort at resistance.

They were required to saddle their horses, each one under guard while doing so. They were then told to mount, a man holding each horse while they complied, then each had his hands tied behind him and a rope fastened his legs under his horse, and thus mounted all was ready for the start.

Chapter XII

They were taken back beyond the eastern end of the cañon to where the train was from which the stock was stolen, and turned over to Mr. Phillips. A guard was placed over them, and a train or two camped further back was notified of their capture.

Next morning there were perhaps fifty men collected from both front and rear trains.

But I forgot to say that, during the night, a posse, or company of four, was sent to the trading post at the entrance to the cañon to arrest two others of their company whose purpose it was to rob the post that night. They were found there, having made arrangements with the keeper to sleep there that night, representing themselves as parties left behind their train looking for some lost cattle. It was no uncommon thing, in case of two or three head escaping the guard, to have some one look through trains following to see if they had fallen in with any of them, as they sometimes did. There was strict honor and honesty among the emigrants that year, at least so far as our observations went. A time or two parties came to our train from before us inquiring if we had lost any of ours, and would go on to the next train or two if not too far ahead, they having picked up some strays.

These men were taken to Phillips' camp and placed under guard with the others.

Next morning a regular court was organized, consisting of judge, jury of twelve and two attorneys, one for prosecuting and one for defending. The case was called, as they were all tried together, it requiring too much time to try them separately. The organizing and trial consumed the entire day until dark, and the Jury were given 'til next morning to bring in their verdict. Of course, they returned to their respective camps to sleep, the judge charging them to discuss the matter with no one and to return in the morning, get together and make up their verdict. They were on hand early and soon had agreed and were ready to return their verdict of "guilty", which was unanimous. During the night one of the attorneys had secured the written confession of one of the two leaders, Lyons and Morgan by name, as given by themselves. They were those who were arrested at the trading post. This confession was written and signed by Morgan in the presence of witnesses and, by permission of the court, was read to the jury before their retiring to make up their verdict.

It was serious, solemn occasion for the judge. There was no question of their guilt, but they could not be turned over to a regular court of law for there was none in possibly hundreds of miles, and there was no way in which they could be secured against further carrying out their avowed purpose of robbing and stealing and possible murder; though up to this time, so far as could be learned, no one had been killed by them, they claimed in their examination that they intended to do their work without killing if they could—but after all to condemn men to death for stealing and robbing only was an extreme penalty. But to turn them loose to prey upon the emigration that was yet to pass along the road was not to be thought of and the court's decision was that the guilty were to be shot.

I say the *guilty*, for the reason that they all cleared one of two brothers, who were sons of respectable parents and members of a wholesale and retail mercantile firm in one of the leading cities of

California at that time, whose names, I presume, have been kept sacredly secret in every recital of the occurrence made in the state by those present at the time.

The judge's decision was approved, so far as I ever knew, universally by those present, of whom there were more than one hundred at the time of its rendering.

Now, I must relate the fact that perhaps there were none present who were not extremely sorry that there was no other way open to deal with them, except to let them go free, but none that I ever heard of heard of, expressed themselves in favor of that. All this had occupied the better part of another day, and the prisoners were given 'til morning to make any preparation they desired. They disposed of their possessions, consisting principally of their outfit, horses, saddles and arms, each one giving what he had to bestow to those to whom they might have taken a passing fancy.

They all went under fictitious, until in their examination they gave what they said were their true names, except one little fellow whose fictitious name was Badger. He declared, when asked his real name, that he would not give it even if he could have his freedom by so doing. He said his were as respectable and respected parents as any man's, and that he would sooner die than that their name should be disgraced by him. And had it been at all appropriate, he would have been cheered to the echo. As it was, a distinct murmur of approval ran through the crowd.

Somehow or somehow else, by hook or by crook, the two leaders managed to escape during the night.

No one, not even the guards, could give any account of how or when they got away.

The next morning each of the four remaining was given the right to choose by whom he should be shot. There was but one refusal, and that was by a young fellow chosen by Badger, who positively refused. The judge then, as Badger would make no further choice, appointed one whom Badger accepted. He certainly was a brave man and did not seem a bad one, but if not, like poor Tray, was caught in bad company and had to pay the penalty.

They were placed in a line, their eyes bandaged, their hands tied behind them and they were made to kneel down. At a given sign, it was almost as if a single shot had been fired, and as if a single man had fallen, so near together was it that they gave up their lives. Graves had already been prepared, as the people gathered were not conditioned to tarry under the circumstances. As soon as decency permitted, they were buried and the crowd dispersed.

The young man that was unanimously cleared by them as refusing, on all occasions, to take part in their raids on stock or otherwise, was taken in charge by Mr. Phillips and returned to his father, so I heard. He was in the start induced to go from California into the mountains on a professed hunt and, when told what their business really was, wanted to return home, but was informed that, should he make the attempt, he would be killed, under which threat he feared to undertake it.

So ends the most important event, as well as the most solemn, that occurred, as I suppose, on the plains that season. So also ends this chapter, as their statements, or rather the sum of them, must be left for another, as they are too long to be told here.

Chapter XIII

The statements of the men agreed quite well with those given in Morgan's confession, so far as I learned what their statements were.

The company was gathered in California entirely, and gave out that they were going to the mountains on a hunting and trapping expedition. Getting well out on the plains, they laid their plans of operation. Having prepared themselves with a counterfeiting outfit, their purpose was, by stealing a few head of cattle or horses from the larger droves, to get enough together to drive to Salt Lake and there dispose of them for material to make counterfeit coin, of which Lewis had for a short time a small specimen.

They had collected one lot and driven there, and disposed of them. They had established headquarters somewhere in the mountains where they kept tools and material stored, while out on their raids and also their stolen stock. At the time of their capture they were gathering their second lot of cattle.

One of their rules, as stated, was never to do any killing, unless it was in fight when on their raids.

It was Lyons and one of the four that was shot that came to our camp with the pitiful story of hunger. It was their purpose, however, to learn how well our camp was protected and what strength of guard was with the stock, as they had, by some means, already learned that the stock were driven some distance away for feed. It so happened that several of the boys were cleaning, oiling and looking after their guns and pistols about the general campfire at the time they came to camp. This, with the number of men present, kept them from an attempt to rob the camp. They had also sent two men to spy out the strength of the guard about the stock.

Seeing so strong a guard, they decided to make no effort to steal any. It was only this timely precaution on the part of our leaders that prevented our having trouble with them. This, however, was only the ordinary custom of the entire trip, and we had never been the wiser of our danger on this occasion had they not told us of it.

This was substantially their statement, with other minor things of little or no interest, and not worth recording here.

Our train in the meantime had been moving on at the usual rate of travel and it took two good days' ride to overtake it. After this nothing worthy of recording occurred until we reached the sink of the Humboldt. This with its very small beginning, if the spring on the summit is its head, had grown into a stream of no mean proportions, and its strange peculiarity is the losing itself in the sands of the dessert, just sinking there, to show itself no more.

At the point where we camped there was not the slightest perceptible current, though the channel was eight feet deep and the banks full. Neither was there sign of stagnation in the water. It was cool, clear, nice water. Leaves and grass were thrown into it and watched without revealing any movement, save as a breeze might drive it one way or another, up, down or across the stream.

It was a good thirty-six hours' drive from there to the Carson River, where we would strike it. This was at an old station or camp of some kind, called in the days of its existence Ragtown. At this time, though, it was entirely wiped off the map and off the ground also, excepting a pole now and then, which possibly had been part of a tent at one time.

We started quite early that we might make as much distance in the cool of the morning as possible, for in this drive there is neither wood, water nor grass. Everything in camp that would hold water so it could be hauled was filled the evening previous, jugs, kegs, canteens, etc., and we were placed on an allowance at that. The horses must have a swallow or two at noon and so must each of the oxen. Of course, even then the poor things suffered, but so did the men also. However, there was no serious suffering with any, either stock or people. About sundown, or a little before, we rested for half an hour, or while we ate something, a piece of bread and meat being about all. Then we started again.

About half past three in the morning a half was called. Most of us were wondering why, as for quite a while the stock, both loose and yoked, had been traveling unusually well. More of the drivers were placed ahead than were kept behind the loose stock.

This, to most of us, was quite mysterious. My team was constantly crowding the one just in front of me, and that being the lead team, required two men to hold it back. On halting, the mystery was explained.

We were within about three miles of Carson River, and the cool morning breeze had brought to them the smell of water. Thirsty as they were, they were anxious to push forward to where their thirst could be satisfied. It took all hands to hold them until daylight, such was their anxiety.

When we started in the morning only two drivers were put behind, and they only to see that no over-tired stragglers were lost.

The reason for holding them from the river until daylight was because willows grew in great abundance on the river, and Indians or other thieves might be there, and in the darkness and among the willows would have opportunity to steal them or kill them on the ground in large numbers.

As before said, it was difficult to hold them at a distance of three miles. On coming within half a mile, they were simply unmanageable, breaking through, running around and almost over, the drivers, rather the holders-back. They made an irresistible rush for the water. Of course, there was no effort made to prevent their going then, as the sun was up; the men scattered up and down the stream, however, keeping a sharp lookout among the willows and on the opposite side of the river.

There was no sign or appearance of Indians, and only the two white men who kept the trading post.

The quite general opinion among the emigrants regarding the trading post men was, that, as Mrs. Partington would say: "They were no better than they ought to be." They would charge any kind of prices they thought necessity would force one to pay.

They bought worn-down cattle, such as were uncertain of travelin' through, and generally got them for a song, and then wanted the other fellow to sing it. If an animal was so worn out that it was certain it could go but little further, they wouldn't give the song for it, even if the owner did sing it, claiming, of course, that it would die, when they and every one knew that all was needed was rest and a little feed.

Chapter XIV

Every one recognized the fact that, at some previous time, those men had been emigrants themselves, and that they well knew it was one of, if not the principal purpose of all who undertook this journey to have an abundance of provisions to do them through. We had sufficient to last us two months after our journey was done. So that the selling of food to emigrants was not to be depended upon as a means of making money.

Hence when a camp was made near a trading post, everybody was on the lookout. On two or three occasions they tried to draw some of the boys into a game of cards, but failed.

After the thirty-six hours' drive across the desert from the Sink, our stock was more tired than at any time on the road. So we drove three or four miles to good feed and rested, starting from Ragtown after our noon lunch, which was short, as we had quite a late breakfast.

Another reason for resting was that in the afternoon of the next day we would have to go through Carson Cañon, and which proved the roughest road of the entire journey, as well as the roughest any of the company had ever seen, save those who had gone through it before.

Unfortunately, that was my day to lead. I found the afternoon, going through the cañon, the worst half day's drive I ever made. The road lay in the bed of the river, which at that season of the year had but little water in it and some places none.

The road bed consisted, almost every foot of the way, of stones and rock from one foot to three feet in diameter, and wagons not in good condition were exceedingly liable to be wrecked. Indeed, careful driving was necessary with the best of them.

Several times, where the rocks stood solidly in the ground and were of such dimensions that the oxen found it difficult to get by them, one either side, and of such height that the front axle would not pass over them, smaller stones would be piled on either side for the wheels to roll up on them and so elevate the axle that it would pass over.

This was both a slow process and hard work, and I am sure there was one glad boy when we got through, and as tired as glad.

Coming out of it, though, we came upon the most delightful scene that had greeted our eyes for many a weary day. A nice open valley, well-built ranch house, green meadows, all presenting the first home scene we had beheld for weeks and months.

The occupants and owners of the ranch, Mr. Sides and Mr. Abernathy, were men with whom my brother had crossed in 1849. They had a fine large stock ranch, well stocked with both horses and cattle, and altogether an inviting and restful scene to eye and body of an emigrant.

We spent the night and next day until noon there. Sides and Abernathy tried hard to persuade Lewis to locate near them, as there was another valley a few miles away, as good as this for stock. As such had not been his plans, he decided to go on across the Sierra Nevadas and into the valleys of California.

These mountains were not only distinctly in view, but seemingly just at hand. In fact, we were in the foothills of the Sierras, of which Carson Cañon was our first and worst experience. They were altogether different in character from what we had seen of the Rockies. There, almost all of what one inexperienced would call mountains were in the distance. There being on the road almost nothing like a mountain, but there was apparently that endless up, up all the while. Frequently on either side were to be seen snow-capped peaks in the distance, some of them appearing to rise until they hid their summits in the very heavens themselves.

The Sierras are there rearing their heads up just before you, pile upon pile, and in length in either direction, mile after mile, farther than the eye can reach, in appearance challenging the most daring wayfarer to attempt their crossing on foot, to say nothing of wagons and teams. Indeed, in those days there was no child's play in the undertaking, while truly it was a task of comparative ease and comfort in proportion to what it looked to be from a distance; in many places it was one of considerable care and anxiety.

Literally, there was no such thing as roads. Just the wheel tracks of wagons of former years. I suppose at this time there had never been a day's work put on it, unless the earlier emigrants, coming to an impassable barrier, stream, gulch or sharp mountain point, some such obstruction as must be overcome to pass at all; there had not been anything done in the way of road work.

We, however, had nothing of the kind to hinder, as those ahead of us had repaired the places needing it. Of course, no one thought of doing anything further than what was actually necessary to let them by a bad place. "Every man for himself" was the universal rule in such cases.

Yet in case of real need, I presume but few places on earth more quickly would develop the fact that the milk of human kindness had not entirely dried up, than on the plains.

This characteristic was fully developed in the case of those robbers, recited in previous pages hereof. You must know it was no small matter, hundreds and hundreds of miles from anywhere, with no certain knowledge of just when you can get there, and every dollar you are worth invested in what you have with you. In many, yes in most, instances, that year, families, women and children—that from the day they leave the borders of civilization until they reach them again are day by day exposed to suffering, danger and death, or worse. I say it is no small thing for train after train to stop and voluntarily loan themselves and their all, and in most instances possibly not for their own good either.

If in a narrative of events it might be allowable briefly to speculate, it might not be so very difficult to ascertain the true reason of this. Nor are we to ascribe that reason in any great degree to mean circumstances. Circumstances have but little influence on human selfishness, of which most are possessed in greater or less degree, unless said circumstances are such as play into the hands of our betterment. I really believe but few places and circumstances have been discovered better adapted to develop selfishness than on the plains.

Why then the other trait referred to? Because in those days, as a rule, they were big hearted, broad minded, whole souled and all around stalwart people, who taking their lives in their hands, as it were, were ready to spend from five to six months under all the trials, tribulations, difficulties, dangers and all the rest of it, in thousands of instances leaving their bodies for coyote's food and their bones to bleach on the sands of the dessert. The other kind came by water.

Chapter XV

Now-a-days, any one with a few dollars may, at the Atlantic seaboard, step aboard a palace car, and with all, or comparatively so, their care for safety, comfort and a general good time thrown upon others, make the trip in five or six days. Not one in a thousand ever takes thought of what these early pioneers underwent to make it possible that they now can take the journey with so much comfort and pleasure.

Still many of them are today boastful to their friends in the East. I have heard them do so to old Californians, of the great deed of valor they had performed in thus making the journey. With little or no appreciation of the dangers and trials of those who came before them, opening the way and the country as well after getting here, and with the almost absolute certainty, if they had appreciated them, would never undertake it, many of them are quite ready to tell the tale of their brave undertaking.

This is not to boast of the bravery of the writer, for as a boy he was just the right age, that his judgment was not sufficient to weigh these difficulties and dangers. Indeed, I have no recollection of their ever entering my mind, either before starting or on the road, save in one or two instances already related. I have crossed several times by rail since, but never had anything like the pleasure I had this first time by ox team.

In crossing the Sierras but one or two things occurred worthy of relation. Twice we came down mountains so steep that all the team but the wheelers were taken loose, and with ropes fastened around the hind axle of the wagon, and also to the yoke ring of the lead yoke, both hind wheels rough locked, with a man to each yoke to make them hold back all they could, we got all the wagons down safely. I was told that, in earlier years, when there was, practically speaking, no road, ropes were fastened to the hind axle, all the cattle but the wheelers taken loose. Then ropes were wrapped around trees, and with men holding them, they were thus let down.

We started in for our climb at what was then known as "Old Mormon Town". They had a fort and quite a settlement there at one time, but it was deserted at this time.

In three or four days we came into the then mining region, and every one felt that sure enough we were in California at last.

The day we passed Hangtown–now Placerville–I was driving loose cattle for a change, and there was some dust in that locality in those days, particularly at the *stub end* of a drove of five hundred cattle, and especially when they were crowded into the narrow street of a small mining town.

Standing on the porch of a house on the brink of a bank of the narrow street was a little girl, perhaps six or seven years old intensely interested in watching the cattle as they passed. How thick the dust settled on me was I do not know, but as I came opposite the child and she noticed me, she threw up her hands, exclaiming at the same time: "La Ma, here's a nigger." The boys said they were not aware before that there was a white "nigger" in the crowd. From that on I was frequently mentioned as the "white nigger."

Well, we are about through our journey; we are off the plains and in California. A day more and we were in the beautiful Sacramento Valley which at that time was but little more than one

great stock ranch. Herd after herd of Spanish cattle were to be
seen as we passed along, among which it was all one's life was,
worth to be caught on foot, though safe to go on horseback.

It was then thought that the valley was unfit for anything like
farming purposes, being as was then thought altogether too dry
for farming, the earlier Americans had fallen in with the Spanish
idea that stock raising was all it was good for. And as far as
memory serves me, I did not see a furrow of plowed ground from
one side of it to the other, except where we camped the first night
at its extreme eastern side.

There a man had plowed a small piece for a garden as, in the
spring, a small stream ran down and he could irrigate an early
garden. He said the whole valley was not worth ten cents only for
stock raising.

How little we know of our own best interests sometimes. Had
that man known what has since been found out, he could in a few
years have made a fortune, even as many did later. All cereals at
that time were selling at from three to four, and even at times for
five, cents per pound. In a few years Sacramento Valley proved
to be the great grain raising section of the state. It is today the
best large body of land in California and will eventually be the
garden spot of the entire coast. Climatically it is not so good as
many other parts, but both climate and soil are such as will grow
almost anything in great abundance, with sufficient water, and
the government is bringing into the valley a very extensive system for irrigation.

However, this is not an advertisement for either Sacramento
Valley or California. So, as much as I would delight in booming
them both, I must leave it all out. And having re-made my journey of fifty-seven years ago, I must soon close these pages. These,
of course, are but few of the many events transpiring during the
journey, but most of the others would probably prove uninterest-
ing.

In presenting these reminiscences, I must remind my readers that they are given wholly from memory, hence not in the order of their occurrence as to time, strictly. In thus briefly sketching my journey, I have, in vision, re-visited not alone the scenes of the occurrences related, but almost every day's journey has been before me, first or last, as I have tried to tell the story of those events given.

Numerous things that have scarcely been recalled since the completion of the trip have again been vividly before me. Whether others shall ever enjoy reading them, it has been a source of great pleasure to me to recall and place them on paper.

Leaving Lafayette County, Missouri, May 7th, 1856, we made the end of our journey at Napa City, then but a small village, on September 13th, of the same year, and were, therefore, four months and six days on the road. Starting as stated at the last end of the emigration leaving Missouri, we were well in front of its middle on arriving at our journey's end.

~J. N. Borroughs

Epilogue

After arriving in California, Joe Borroughs continued his active
and productive life. At eighteen, he took his first pastorate. In
1862, at twenty-two, he married Elizabeth McKinley in Healdsburg. He took her to Upper Lake where he was already a school
teacher and the pastor of the Baptist church. He pastored in Lake
and Sonoma Counties, had charge of most of the Baptist churches,
and taught school in every town in the county. He and Elizabeth
had eight children–seven daughters and a son. After he retired,
the couple settled in Oakland where, in 1912, they celebrated
their Golden Wedding Anniversary. He died in 1919 at the age of
seventy-nine. Somewhere in Oakland, California in a Baptist
Church, there is a stained glass window dedicated to this beloved
pioneer pastor.

Scrapbook

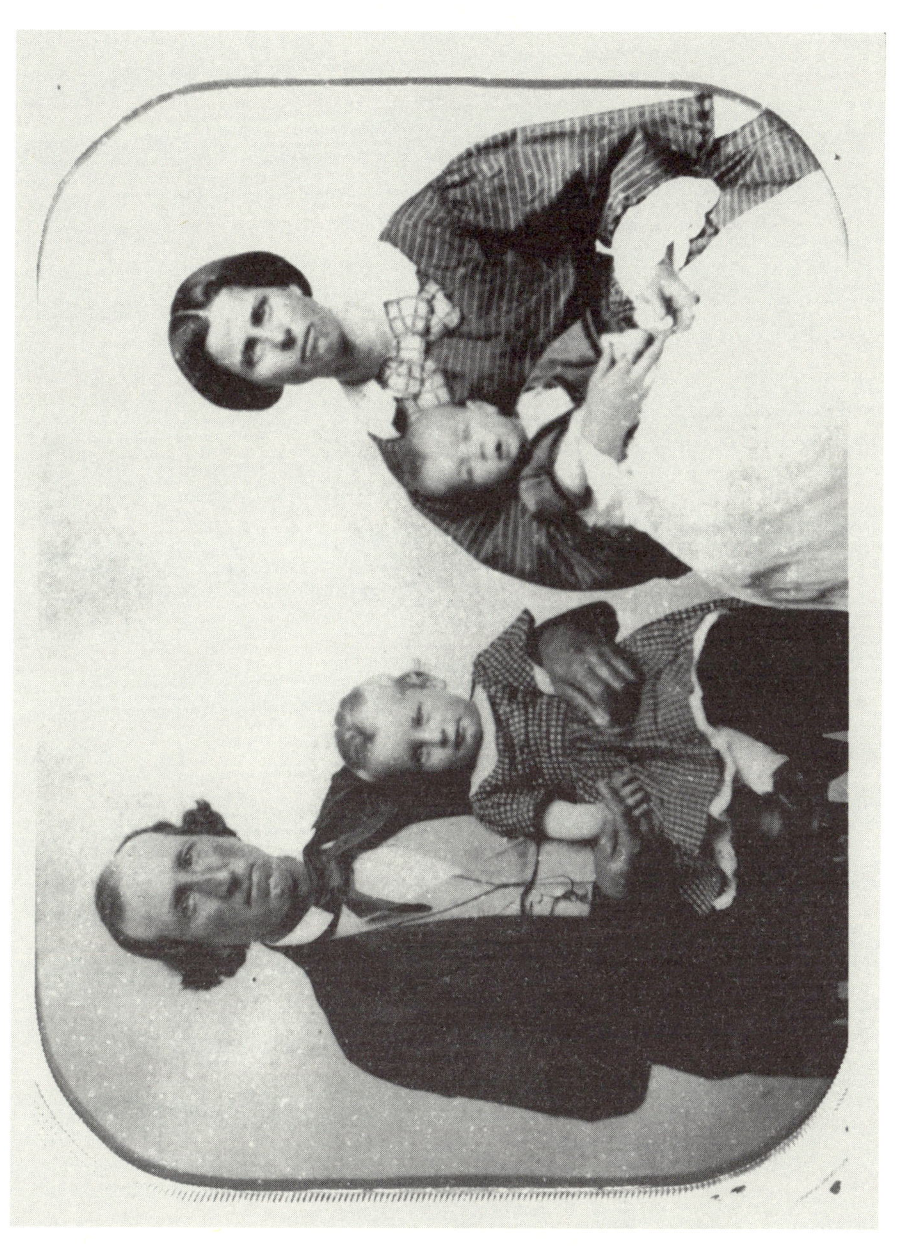

*Lewis Chamblee Borroughs with Sarah Ann Johnson
and their children Francis Henrietta (left)
and Richard Bryan (right)*

Contracts Book D.

State of Missouri }
County of Lafayette }

I the undersigned a justice of the Peace of Sniabar Township in Lafayette County do certify that I united in marriage on the 11th day of May 1856 Lewis Borroughs and Sarah Ann Johnson both of Lafayette County State of Mo.

This July the 20nd 1856

Isaac N. Bledsoe J. P.

Filed & Recorded August 2nd 1856

S.W. Smallwood Clerk

By C.B. Daniel Deputy

STATE OF MISSOURI,
COUNTY OF __Lafayette__ } ss.

I, __Robert Dryer__ Recorder of Deeds in and for said County, hereby certify that the above is a true copy of the original __Marriage Record__ as the same appears __in Book D Page 259__ in my office.

WITNESS my hand as Recorder, and the seal of my office. Done at office in __Lexington, Missouri__, this __10th__ day of __August__ 19__70__.

__Robert Dryer__ Clerk.

Per ____________________ Deputy Recorder

(Top) Original Marriage License of
Lewis Chamblee Borroughs and Sarah Ann Johnson
May 11, 1856, Lafayette County, Lexington Missouri

(Bottom) Certification of veracity of hand written Marriage License
August 10, 1970, Lafayette County, Lexington Missouri

Rev. J. N. Borroughs and Mrs. Borroughs, who celebrated their golden wedding anniversary at their Alameda home.

Many Guests Are Entertained at the Home of Rev. J. N. Borroughs in Alameda

OAKLAND, November 3.—Seated beneath a canopy of California poppies and chrysanthemums, their faces wreathed in smiles of appreciation at the reception they were receiving from scores of friends and relatives, Rev. Mr. and Mrs. J. N. Burroughs celebrated the golden jubilee of their wedded life last night at the home of their daughter, Mrs. Carrie Hall, 322 Howard street, Piedmont. The aged couple, who have lived in this State for over half a century, were also the recipients of hundreds of telegrams and messages of congratulation from well wishers in this State and Eastern and Northern States of the Union.

The reception was attended by 100 persons. The rooms of the house were filled with a profusion of golden flowers, emblematic of the occasion, and the gowns of many of the guests were in harmony with the scheme of decoration. At the banquet the couple were further tendered felicitations and good wishes of the guests in appropriate toasts. A programme of literary and musical numbers was given. Rev. William Keeney Towner, pastor of the First Baptist Church of this city, recited a poem and sang a solo. Mrs. Edith Reavis and Miss Awana rendered solos, the latter vocalist accompanying her songs, sung in the native Hawaiian tongue, on the ukulele. Mrs. R. H. Mahoney completed the programme with a specially selected recitation.

Dr. J. N. Borroughs is 72 years of age and is said to be the oldest Baptist minister in the State from a point of view of service. He came to California with an older brother in 1856 from Anderson, South Carolina. He was preceded by his future wife, Miss Elizabeth McKinley, by three years. In 1862 the couple were wedded in Healdsburg, Sonoma county, in which place Dr. Borroughs assumed his first pastorate at the age of 18 years. For many years he held pastorates in Lake county and other counties in Northern California and was a well-known figure in Baptist denominational circles.

For the past eight years Dr. Borroughs has retired from active service and made his home at 949 Thirty-fourth street, Oakland. Eight children were born to the couple, seven daughters and one son, the latter, J. N. Borroughs Jr., being a prominent business man of Oakland.

Newspaper clipping of Reverend and Mrs. Joseph Newton Borroughs' 50th Wedding Anniversary celebration

PIONEER COUNTY MINISTER PASSES AWAY

Rev. J. N. Borroughs, a pioneer minister and teacher of Lake county, ended his earthly career in the county he loved so well and where so many of his early experiences were met, The death occurred at Saratoga Springs on Monday. Rev. Borroughs had been there but a few days, coming with his daughter Mrs. Hall for the benefit of his health. He had been a sufferer from kidney and heart trouble for several months.

Rev. Borroughs was well known to many of the older residents of Lake county. He was born in Anderson, South Carolina December 25th, 1840, making his age at death 79 years, 6 months and 9 days. He came to California in his 14th year, in 1856, with his older brother Louis, who was the father of R. B. Burriss. Brothers in the same family spelled their name differently.

J. N. Burroughs came to Lake county when 22 years old. He had begun his ministerial work at the age of 18. Marrying Miss Elizabeth McKinley of Healdsburg on October 14th, 1862, he took her as a bride to Upper Lake, where he was then pastor of the Baptist church and also taught school. During his young manhod he had charge of most of the Baptist churches, and taught school in every town, in the county.

Following his departure from Lake county, Rev. Borroughs became well know and prominent thruout the State, having held pastorates in fourteen of the northern counties. He retired several years ago, and had since made his home in Oakland, where in 1912 he and his wife celebrated their golden wedding anniversary. His life mate was called to her Heavenly home three years ago.

He was the father of seven daughters and one son, four of whom remain to mourn his death. They are Mrs. Carrie E. Hall, Mrs. Arch Currie, Mrs. J. E. Trewhitt and J. N. Borroughs, Jr., all of Oakland Grandchildren are Mrs. Kenneth Gillis and Mrs. William Rogers of Fresno, Mrs. Frank Hoard of Modesto, Mrs. Ford Stidham, Archie Currie and Melville Sample of Oakland. Also four great-grandchildren survive this estimable man. He was the uncle of Mrs. Fannie Gruwell, R. B. Burriss and Mrs. Chester White.

The body was prepared for burial and sent to Oakland by F. D. Sweet. Mr. Burriss and Mrs. Gruwell attended the funeral in that city.

Newspaper clipping of
Reverend Joseph Newton Borroughs' obituary